FINANCIAL
TRANSFORMATION

STOP JUGGLING YOUR DEBT AND BECOME FINANCIALLY FIT!

MARSHEA MAYFIELD

FINANCIAL TRANSFORMATION:

Stop Juggling Your Debt and Become Financially Fit!

Marshea Mayfield

Unless otherwise indicated, all scripture references
are taken from the King James Version of the
Bible.

FINANCIAL SERVICES PLUS LLC
711 Azalea Dr., Waynesboro, MS 39367
www.FinancialServicesPlusLLC.com

ISBN: 978-1508807216

For Information, Contact:

Pearly Gates Publishing LLC
P.O. Box 671086
Houston, TX 77067
info@AngAccAdminSvcs.com

Printed in United States of America
by CreateSpace

Dedication

This book is dedicated to my five lovely children:
Joseph McFarland, Timothy Stokes,
Timeria Stokes, Mikeria Stokes,
and Makanli Mayfield. I pray that one day this
guide might serve as a roadmap for success as you
embrace your own financial journeys.

Acknowledgements

To Tyrone, my loving husband: Thank you for your love and patience. Your belief and support allows me to chase after my dreams. I am so grateful to share this journey with you!

To my Pastor, Bobbie Graham-Ashley, who has been a mother, sister, leader, and friend; my sisters, Kristy Chambers and Erica Williamson; father, Lonnie Chambers; my mother (Rest In Peace), Priscilla Avery-Chambers; family, spiritual family, and friends – thank you for your continued love and support.

To the Financial Services Plus team: Hats off to you! You guys are my backbone, and I am grateful to have such a supportive team.

To my Accountability Partner, Tarsha Calhoun, I love and thank God for you!

Last, but not least: To you, my lovely clients who have supported me since day one – I love and appreciate you!

Table of Contents

Dedication	7
Acknowledgements	8
Welcome	10
My Story	13
This Program is for You If	16
Client Testimonial #1	18
Goal Planner	19
More of My Story	22
Client Testimonial #2	24
Money Attitudes from Your Childhood	25
Track your Spending	27
Budget Worksheet #1	31
Budget Worksheet #2	40
Face It	42
Do It Yourself Credit Repair	44
Dealing with Harassing Creditors	47
Do It Yourself Credit Dispute	50
You Are A Winner	54
Additional Budget Worksheets	55

WELCOME! WELCOME! WELCOME!

Are you asking, "*What are the benefits to be gained from the 90-Day Financial Fit program?*"

Let me explain…

1. **Together**, we will maximize every dollar earned and create a financial plan to take control of your money so you will no longer live paycheck to paycheck.
2. **We** will implement a system to rapidly eliminate your debt.
3. **You** will complete the course that will teach you the fundamentals of money management and help you establish wise financial habits.

Financial Services Plus LLC is compassionate and sincere when it comes to your family's financial prosperity. Coaching services are not judgmental; instead, it is encouraging and *always* confidential. I believe it is my responsibility to help you achieve your financial goals.

Now, let's figure out what has happened with your finances that has landed you in your current situation of not being **financially fit**! Don't be afraid to explore the truth about money.

Someone once asked me the question, "Why do you offer a Financial Fit program?" My answer was simple: "It's my testimony." I am a living witness that with proper planning and determination, you can overcome any obstacle.

My Story

That feeling of being on top of the world is *amazing*! I was happy with my life, income, and the outlook for my future. I had a job I liked (*not loved*), made really good money, and was a wife and mother of three. You could say I was comfortable – living the American dream. My husband and I purchased a new home in a neighborhood that wasn't very accepting of 'my kind'. I was driving the car of my choice and my children had the things they desired. Well, all of that changed in the blink of an eye.

After working on my job for over eight years, I was told that in 14 days my services would no longer be needed. I was devastated and afraid! I went home that day to share the news with my husband with the hope that he would support the family during this difficult time. Long story short: It didn't work out like that.

We divorced, and I was forced to take care of my family with absolutely no income. I became frustrated with trying to make ends meet and became a pro at robbing Peter to pay Paul.

The worst thing of all is that I maintained the appearance that all things in my life were great. I dressed nice, my kids were always well-groomed, and I continued to live in my dream home – but on the inside, I was dying.

I often referred to myself as a clown during this time. I juggled my bills daily to see what I could afford to pay, which ones I could avoid for a moment, and which ones were the most important. My mind goes back to when my daughter would be so happy to check the mail. She would run through the door with a high level of excitement saying, "Mommy, I have the mail!" I would put on the clown face and simply reply, "Thanks, hun!" Meanwhile on the inside, I was crying.

Who do I owe now? Who is threatening to take something now? I was so bold, I would make comments like, "They can't get blood from a turnip!" or "They will get it when they get it." or how about, "Add it to the top of the pile at the Credit Bureau." I was really fooling myself! I got tired of being sick and tired. The foreclosure notice on my front door was the straw that broke the camel's back. I took action!

Let me share with you the steps that allowed me to save my home, increase my credit score, and release my financial frustration.

This program is for you if:

➢ You don't know where to begin with your finances

➢ You want to learn how to save and spend money properly

➢ Your debt is out of control

➢ You are living paycheck to paycheck

➢ You lack a concrete plan to manage your finances

➢ You need assistance to reach your financial goals

➢ You need honest and straightforward advice

➢ You need someone to hold your

hand through the process

➢ You had a drastic change in your

finances and you need help

changing your living arrangements

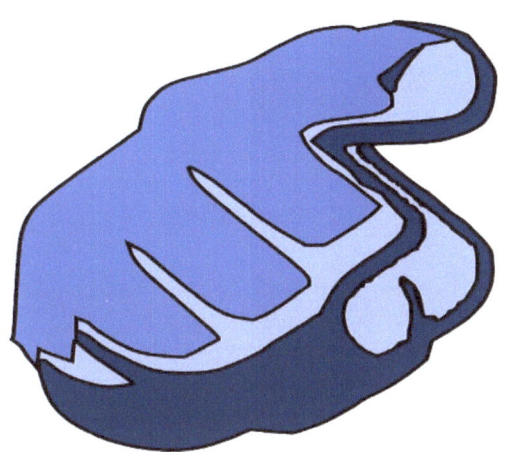

Client Testimonial #1

"I just want to thank you for offering the 4-week **Financial Fit** training. The training allowed me to sit down and write down my goals that I had swarming around my head.

"The training also taught me to put the goals in realistic time frames and to find ways to execute them monetarily. I was never one to track my expenses on a daily basis – even though I was told to do so in the past.

The training served as accountability and support. I realized there are others on the same path as myself that want to hit those markers in life rather than just talking about it.

Thanks for helping me kick the procrastination with my finances out the door!"

~ S. Callis

Financial Services Plus LLC Goal Planner

Take a moment to answer each of the following questions truthfully and honestly:

1. How do you feel about your current financial situation?

_____
_____
_____

2. What would you like to change about your current financial situation?

_____
_____
_____
_____
_____

3. Are your expenses currently more than your income?
YES NO
List your expenses below.

_____
_____
_____
_____
_____
_____
_____

4. What debt will you eliminate?

_____
_____
_____
_____
_____
_____
_____
_____

5. Are you happy with your current career/job? YES or NO

What would you like to change?

_____
_____
_____
_____

6. What does living a financially fit lifestyle look like to you?

_____
_____
_____
_____
_____
_____
_____

7. List 5 personal or business goals.

_____
_____
_____
_____
_____
_____
_____
_____

8. Are you living your life to the fullest?
   YES or NO

9. Do you require your worth from your
   employer/business?
   YES or NO

If you answered "YES" to **ANY** of the above questions, then you are in the right place! I am here to help you obtain your financial goals.

More of My Story...

Several years ago, I was a victim of Internet fraud. My husband and I were contacted by an adoption agency to adopt a young lady from Africa. We were truly excited as we took all of the necessary precautions to ensure we were doing what was right and legal. Nevertheless, we were scammed out of **$16,000**. We exhausted our savings and began spending our personal funds in the hopes of rescuing the young lady.

This situation caused us to get behind in our monthly expenditures, leading to foreclosure notices on our door, phones ringing off the hook, and many bills were unopened due to the frustration of not being in a position to pay. I was more embarrassed because I was a person that others depended on to assist with their financial frustrations and yet, there I was!

I vowed that I would not stay in that situation and began developing a plan. In six months, we were finally financially free!

Client Testimonial #2

"I just wanted to say thank you for the awesome 4-week challenge. I went in not expecting to gain much and came out so aware and ready to make some much-needed changes.

"Writing down my goals helped me to pull my thoughts together, put a plan in place, and begin executing that plan to reach my goals. It is nice to be able to keep track of my progression towards each goal as well.

"The weekly expense tracking was very eye-opening as I am not a lover of budgets. It also opened the door for much-needed communication with my husband. I'm amazed at how quickly we both were able to get on the same page. This is just one more area that I feel God has strengthened our marriage.

"Having an accountability partner within the group was nice. It kept me motivated and engaged knowing I was teamed up with someone working towards their goals as well.

"I feel empowered and confident to keep working towards becoming financially healthy. Thank you for the support!" ~ S. Timmons

Money Attitudes from Your Childhood

What was your life like as a child? How do your past experiences affect your life now? Let's explore some of your childhood memories regarding money. (*This will be a tremendous payoff. You will learn to have less stress and confusion, while gaining a deeper understanding of yourself and the way you fit into the world.*)

Childhood money issues affect every aspect of our lives.

Circle three words that instantly come to mind when you think of money as a child.

Deprived	Poor	Lucky
Rich	Satisfied	Smart
Uninterested	Ignorant	Reward
Controlled	Warned	Dependent
Oblivious		

Why did you choose those 3 words to describe your childhood?

_____
_____
_____
_____
_____

How is the way you handle money similar to your parents?

_____
_____
_____
_____
_____

Track Your Spending

Daydreaming can be really exciting, but very daunting if you're not sure how to achieve your goals. This is where proper planning comes in to play.

Most financial worries come from lack of planning, not lack of money. The primary step to living financially fit is to begin tracking your spending. Tracking may feel time consuming, but when you take time to do it, you gain a much clearer understanding of what you need to do to transform your finances. The following steps will help guide you through that part.

1. Record all of your spending this week, even if it's minor - like buying a pack of gum or putting change in a parking meter. Write down **every** item you buy and its cost.

2. Categorize your list. At the end of the week organize what you spent into 2 groups: Essential (needed) and Non-Essential (not needed).
3. Cross out. Cross out any items you can do without. You may be surprised at expenditures you didn't notice before.

PLEASE NOTE: *I'm only asking you to track for* *one* *week, but to gain a clearer picture of your spending habits, try tracking for a whole month.*

You must face your current situation. This is where you will utilize the next Budget Worksheet. At this point, I encourage you to pull those bills from the drawers, cabinets, etc. (**NOTE:** Don't forget those bills you have "casted away"!) You will need pay stubs for both you and your spouse (if married).

Fill out the following worksheet thoroughly. Once you are clear about all of your expenditures, you can create a solid budget. Please don't let the word "budget" scare you. A budget, simply put, is a plan. It's your plan to success. You will begin to appreciate the amount of stress and frustration that will be alleviated from your life once you honestly face your situation.

This is only the beginning to transforming your finances. It's time for you to stop robbing Peter to pay Paul. It's time-out for showing up as a clown. Your smile will be genuine and true. Your bank account will live up to your painted smile. You will no longer juggle your debt. You will control it!

FINANCIAL SERVICES PLUS LLC

"Financially Fit"
Budget Worksheet #1

www.FinancialServicesPlusLLC.com

SELF:

INCOME: _____

Taxes Paid: _____

Net Income (bring home): _____

SPOUSE:

INCOME: _____

Taxes Paid: _____

Net Income (bring home): _____

1. Are you aware of the amount of taxes you pay per pay period? YES or NO
2. Should you increase or decrease the amount of taxes you pay per pay period?   YES or NO

MONTHLY EXPENSES:

List of Expenses	Amounts Due	List of Expenses	Amounts Due
MORTAGE		FOOD	
LIGHTS		TITHES	
WATER		CHILD CARE	
AUTO			
AUTO INSURANCE			
GAS			
INTERNET			
CABLE			
MORTAGE INS			

Total Expenses:_____

Income _____ - _____ Expenses

=_____Savings

Expenses that are ignored - for the moment:

Now that you've completed the Budget Worksheet, there are some things you must do. It's time to stop overspending and gain control of your finances. Before you construct a budget, there are some things you should do **first**:

> ➤ *Stop incurring new debt.* Borrowing money for consumer spending is no way to make your budget work. You have to put away those credit cards to create a realistic spending plan.

> *Live on a cash basis.* Get used to buying with cash. There is a place for credit card life. For now, don't use them while you're getting used to your new lifestyle.

> *Get a handle on your situation.* Sit down with your monthly bills, statements, checkbook, and everything relating to your household finances. Note due dates and calculate your expenditures for food costs, contributions, tithing, savings, fuel, etc.

> *Organize it.* You should have all of your documents on hand. It is vital to operate in your fullness. You must get it together! You will need the following supplies: hanging folders, file folders, and a plastic tote or filing cabinet. Create files such as: legal documents, tax returns, financial accounts, income, insurance, loans, debts, repairs, etc.

➢ *Fix it.* Now, let's break down your specific plan. Once you are specific, realistic, and detailed, you can begin to take action.

On the Budget Worksheet, you should see if you are living within your means. Did your income exceed your expenses? If so, what's on your list that can be paid off?

_____

_____

_____

_____

What's on your list that is a want?

_____

_____

_____

_____

Which company(ies) can you contact to negotiate with to request a due date change?

_____

_____

_____

_____

_____

NOTE: Changing due dates may be all you need to make accurate and timely payments. This is normally an easy process and only requires a small amount of time on the phone or computer.

Now, let's complete Budget Worksheet #2. It is designed for a 4-week pay period (you can combine columns if you are paid bi-weekly or monthly). At the top, note your monthly income. Now you can begin to create your personal budget.

EXAMPLE (List of bills):

Mortgage: $1,000 – due 1st

Auto Insurance: $300 – due 15th

Auto Payment: $500 – due 1st

Cellular Phone: $200 – due 30th

Electric: $300 – due 15th

Cable: $100 – due 25th

Food: $200

Tithes: $300

TOTAL: $2,900

Following is an example for a person who is paid bi-weekly. For the purposes of this exercise, I chose to have all bills due by the

15th for Week One with a monthly income of $3,500.

Week 1 Paycheck: $1,750	Week 2 Paycheck: $1,750
Mortgage $1,000	Food $100
Insurance $300	Tithes $350
Auto Payment $250 (this is a situation where you can request a date change)	Cell Phone $200
Food $100	Electric $300
Savings $15	Cable $100
Cash in Pocket $75	Auto Payment $250
Total $1,750	Savings $200
(Should be detailed to	Cash in pocket $250
the penny)	**Total $1,750**

Again, that was only an example. The demonstration is to give you a realistic guide. *Your* budget should be realistic, detailed, and specific.

Affirm: "I am creating my own financial destiny."

Scripture

2 Kings 4:7

"The she came and told the man of God. And he said, "Go, sell the oil and pay your debt, and you and your sons can live on the rest.""

Financial Services Plus LLC

"Financially Fit"
Budget Worksheet #2

www.FinancialServicesPlusLLC.com

Week 1	Week 2	Week 3	Week 4
TOTAL:	TOTAL:	TOTAL:	TOTAL:
BALANCE:	BALANCE:	BALANCE:	BALANCE:

What amount will you vow to save each week? (Choose only one.)

$5.00 $10.00

*Additional Budget Worksheets for future logging of finances are located in the back of the book.

(*This weekly budget will allow you to have complete control of your income. If for any reason you stray from this weekly budget, please consult with your financial coach. Control your money. Stop allowing your money to control you!*)

Face It!

➤ Stop the excuses.

It doesn't help to blame others for our mistakes, failures, and bad decisions.

➤ Stop the whining.

Whiners lay in bed thinking it will go away. Whiners take no action. Whiners dwell in the past.

➤ Answer the calls.

Stop dodging those 800 #s. It's time to pay the piper. Most times, once you speak to the creditor, they are willing to work with you. All they want is to communicate!

➤ Open your mail.

Stop storing it in those hidden places. You just may have an offer you can't refuse waiting to be addressed!

➤ Organize it.

Create a filing system so that you can have access to your legal financial statements.

Affirm: "I am releasing and letting go of my money issues."

Scripture
Psalm 23:1

"The Lord is my Shepherd. I shall not want."

Do It Yourself Credit Repair

What should be on my Credit Report?

- ➢ Personal info such as name, phone numbers, address, date of birth, current and previous employers.
- ➢ Credit inquiries – which is when a third party such as a creditor, potential lender, or insurer pulls your credit report. This can remain on your credit for up to two years.
- ➢ Public records obtained from government sources including bankruptcies, tax liens, collections, past due child support, and judgments.

What really affects my credit score?

- ➢ Payment History

Late payments will cause a huge drop in credit rating.

- ➢ Credit History

It's great to have positive lines of credit. If your payment history is good, there is no need to call and cancel the card – but don't accrue new credit.

- ➢ Inquiries

Creditors view this as you are living within your credit means – not your means of income. The more you apply, the more is affects your credit score.

- ➢ Total Debt

Your total debt ratio affects your credit score. It simply says you are in over your head. You owe more than you make.

How do I increase my credit score?

- ➢ Follow your detailed budget.

- ➢ Make monthly payments on time.

- ➢ Transfer high interest rate cards.

- ➢ Stop using credit cards.

- ➢ Negotiate lower interest rates.

Are you being harassed by your creditors?

Fair Debt Collection Practices Act Section 806(5) prohibits the creditors from harassing, annoying, and abusing their authorities. If you are being harassed, I suggest you:

1. Answer calls from your creditors and negotiate an amount that is affordable.
2. Make notes of the harassing calls including dates, names, ID, etc.
3. Notify the creditor by certified mail (following is a sample copy of a form that can be used for this purpose).

Letter to Harassing Creditor
(*Remove that line before sending*)

Your Name
Your Address
Your Town, State, Zip

Name of Harassing Creditor
Their Address
City, State, Zip

Date

Dear Harasser (change to name of Creditor),

Please be advised that on the following dates, _____, I requested that your representative stop calling me at (home/work). This is a form of harassment. I am aware that I have a financial obligation to your company. However, I am unable to meet your obligations due to my financial situation.

I am exercising my rights granted by the Bureau of Consumer Protection – a division of the Federal Trade Commission. I request that no one from your company call my (home/job) again.

You may contact me via U.S. Postal Service at the address noted above. Thank you in advance.

Sincerely,

Your Signature
Your Name

*(**Please note**: You must have documentation that the creditor has called you more times than the normal call cycle AND you must feel and prove this is a form of harassment.)*

FINANCIAL SERVICES PLUS LLC

www.FinancialServicesPlusLLC.com

Do It Yourself Credit Dispute

➢ You can get one free credit report from each of the three major credit bureaus (TransUnion, Equifax, and Experian) once every 12 months from www.annualcreditreport.com. However, the sites do not provide credit scores or, more specifically, FICO® Scores.

➢ It doesn't cost anything to dispute mistakes or outdated items on your credit report. Both the credit reporting company and the information provider (the person, company, or organization that provides information about you to a credit reporting company) are responsible for correcting inaccurate or incomplete information in your report. To take advantage of all your rights, contact both the credit reporting company and the information provider.

➤ Your letter should clearly identify each item in your report you dispute, state the facts and explain why you dispute the information, and request that it be removed or corrected. You may want to disclose a copy of your report with the items in question circled.

➤ Send your letter by certified mail with "Return Receipt Requested" so that you can document when the credit reporting company received the documentation. Remember to include copies of the applicable enclosures and save copies for your files.

➤ An example of a dispute letter follows.

Sample Dispute Letter to Credit Bureaus

[Your Name]
[Your Address]
[Your City, State, Zip]

[Date]

Complaint Department
[Company Name]
[Street Address]
[City, State, Zip]

Dear Sir or Madam:

I am writing to dispute the following information in my file. I have circled the items I dispute on the attached copy of the report I received.

This item **[identify item(s) disputed by name of source, such as creditors or tax court, and identify type of item, such as credit account, judgment, etc.]** is **[inaccurate or incomplete]** because **[describe what is inaccurate or incomplete and why]**. I am requesting that the item be removed **[or request another specific change]** to correct the information.

Enclosed are copies of **[use this sentence (if applicable) to describe any enclosed documentation, such as payment records and court documents]** supporting my position. Please reinvestigate this **[these]** matter**[s]** and **[delete or correct]** the disputed item**[s]** as soon as possible.

Sincerely,

Your Signature
Your name

YOU ARE A WINNER!

- ➢ WINNERS TAKE ACTION!
- ➢ WINNERS DON'T MAKE EXCUSES!
- ➢ WINNERS DON'T DWELL ON THE PAST!
- ➢ WINNERS DON'T LAY IN BED THINKING IT WILL GO AWAY!

Budget Worksheet #2

www.FinancialServicesPlusLLC.com

Week 1	Week 2	Week 3	Week 4
TOTAL:	TOTAL:	TOTAL:	TOTAL:
BALANCE:	BALANCE:	BALANCE:	BALANCE:

Budget Worksheet #2

www.FinancialServicesPlusLLC.com

Week 1	Week 2	Week 3	Week 4
TOTAL:	TOTAL:	TOTAL:	TOTAL:
BALANCE:	BALANCE:	BALANCE:	BALANCE:

Budget Worksheet #2

www.FinancialServicesPlusLLC.com

Week 1	Week 2	Week 3	Week 4
TOTAL:	TOTAL:	TOTAL:	TOTAL:
BALANCE:	BALANCE:	BALANCE:	BALANCE:

Budget Worksheet #2

www.FinancialServicesPlusLLC.com

Week 1	Week 2	Week 3	Week 4
TOTAL:	TOTAL:	TOTAL:	TOTAL:
BALANCE:	BALANCE:	BALANCE:	BALANCE:

Budget Worksheet #2

www.FinancialServicesPlusLLC.com

Week 1	Week 2	Week 3	Week 4
TOTAL:	TOTAL:	TOTAL:	TOTAL:
BALANCE:	BALANCE:	BALANCE:	BALANCE:

Budget Worksheet #2

www.FinancialServicesPlusLLC.com

Week 1	Week 2	Week 3	Week 4
TOTAL:	TOTAL:	TOTAL:	TOTAL:
BALANCE:	BALANCE:	BALANCE:	BALANCE:

Budget Worksheet #2

www.FinancialServicesPlusLLC.com

Week 1	Week 2	Week 3	Week 4
TOTAL:	TOTAL:	TOTAL:	TOTAL:
BALANCE:	BALANCE:	BALANCE:	BALANCE:

NOTES | GOALS | DEADLINES

_____

_____

_____

_____

_____

_____

_____

_____

_____

_____

_____

_____

_____

_____

_____

_____

www.ingramcontent.com/pod-product-compliance
Lightning Source LLC
Chambersburg PA
CBHW040842180526
45159CB00001B/278